LAUGHING MATTERS

FOOD JOKES

Compiled by Pam Rosenberg
Illustrated by Patrick Girouard

Special thanks to Katie Cottrell for her assistance in compiling source materials.

Published in the United States of America by The Child's World®
PO Box 326, Chanhassen, MN 55317-0326
800-599-READ
www.childsworld.com

Acknowledgments

The Child's World®: Mary Berendes, Publishing Director

Editorial Directions, Inc.: E. Russell Primm, Editorial Director and Line
Editor; Katie Marsico, Assistant Editor; Matthew Messbarger, Editorial
Assistant; Susan Ashley, Proofreader

The Design Lab: Kathleen Petelinsek, Designer; Kari Thornborough,
Page Production

Library of Congress Cataloging-in-Publication Data
Rosenberg, Pam.
  Food jokes / compiled by Pam Rosenberg ; illustrated by Patrick Girouard.
      p. cm. — (Laughing matters)
  ISBN 1-59296-279-3 (library bound : alk. paper) 1. Food—Juvenile humor.
2. Riddles, Juvenile. I. Girouard, Patrick. II. Title. III. Series.
  PN6231.F66R67 2005
  818'.602—dc22   2004016859

BREAD AND GRAIN JOKES

Why was the stale loaf of bread arrested?
It tried to get fresh.

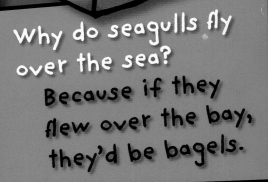

What do you get when you put three ducks in a box?
A box of quackers.

Why do seagulls fly over the sea?
Because if they flew over the bay, they'd be bagels.

Why did the lazy man want a job in the bakery?
So he could loaf around.

How do you keep a bagel from getting away?
You put lox on it.

3

Daniel: Why is this bread full of holes?
School Cook: Because it's whole wheat bread.

City Kid: Do you like raisin bread?
Farmer: Don't know. Never raised any.

DAIRY JOKES

What do cows give after an earthquake?
Milk shakes.

What do dogs put on their pizza?
Mutts-arella cheese.

Did you hear the joke about the butter?
I'd better not tell you because you might spread it around.

What do you call cheese that isn't yours?
Nacho cheese.

What happens when you tell an egg a joke?
It cracks up.

Why did the boy throw butter out the window?
He wanted to see a butterfly.

What do you get when you cross a cow and a duck?
Milk and quackers.

5

What do you get from a pampered cow?
Spoiled milk.

What do outlaws eat with their milk?
Crookies.

What kind of egg did the bad chicken lay?
A deviled egg.

FRUIT AND VEGETABLE JOKES

What would you get if you crossed a sheep and a banana?
A baa-nana.

Why did the man stare at the can of orange juice?
Because it said "concentrate."

What vegetable is dangerous to have on a boat?
A leek.

How do you make a strawberry shake?
Take it to a scary movie.

How do you fix a cracked pumpkin?
With a pumpkin patch.

Why did the lettuce blush?
It saw the salad dressing.

School Cook: Eat your vegetables. Green things are good for you.
Anna: Okay. Then I'll have some pistachio ice cream.

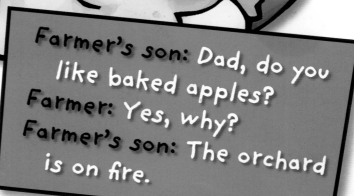

Farmer's son: Dad, do you like baked apples?
Farmer: Yes, why?
Farmer's son: The orchard is on fire.

8

Knock Knock.
Who's there?
Lettuce.
Lettuce who?
Lettuce in, it's cold outside!

What did one banana sitting in the sun say to the other banana sitting in the sun?
I don't know about you, but I'm starting to peel.

What kind of lettuce was served on the Titanic?
Iceberg lettuce.

What do you call two banana peels?
A pair of slippers.

What did the banana do when it heard the ice scream?
It split.

What's small and yellow and wears a mask?
The Lone Lemon.

What did one strawberry say to the other?
If you weren't so fresh, we wouldn't be in this jam!

What is brown and hairy and wears sunglasses?
A coconut on its summer vacation.

9

What's bright orange and sounds like a parrot?
A carrot.

How do you fix a broken tomato?
With tomato paste.

If a carrot and a cabbage ran a race, who would win?
The cabbage, because it's a head.

Why couldn't the magician tell his magic secrets in the garden?
Because the corn has ears and the potatoes have eyes.

How do you turn soup into gold?
Put 14 carrots in it.

Why did everyone at the party like Mr. Mushroom?
Because he was a fungi.

Did you hear about the banana that snored?
He woke up the whole bunch.

Why couldn't the orange finish the race? It ran out of juice.

What would you get if you crossed a sweet potato with a jazz musician? Yam sessions.

How do you know carrots are good for your eyes? Because you never see rabbits wearing glasses.

What was the nearsighted chicken doing in the farmer's garden? She was sitting on an eggplant.

Why did Tony go out with a prune? Because he couldn't find a date.

If an apple a day keeps the doctor away, what does an onion a day do? It keeps everybody away.

How do you tease fruit? Bananananananana.

11

A man walks into the doctor's office. He has a cucumber up his nose, a carrot in his left ear, and a banana in his right ear. "What's the matter with me?" he asks the doctor. The doctor replies, "You're not eating properly!"

SWEETS AND SNACK JOKES

How does the gingerbread man make his bed?
   With cookie sheets.

What do you get if you cross chocolate candy with a sheep?
   A Hershey-baa.

What kind of candy would a doomed prisoner like to have before he is hanged?
   A Life Saver.

What do you call a person who can drink soda and sing at the same time?
   A pop singer.

MEAT AND FISH JOKES

What has bread on both sides and frightens easily?
A chicken sandwich.

What did the pork chop say to the steak? Nice to meat you.

What did one hot dog say to another? Hi, Frank!

Why did the fried chicken cross the road? Because he saw a fork up ahead.

What do you call a cow with no legs? Ground beef.

Why do fish avoid computers?
They don't want to get caught in the Internet.

How do you make an elephant sandwich?
First, get a very large loaf of bread . . .

What is an astronaut's favorite sandwich?
Launch meat.

What did Mary have at the cookout?
Everyone knows that Mary had a little lamb.

What do cats call mice on skateboards?
Meals on wheels.

What's the worst thing about being an octopus?
Washing your hands before dinner.

What did the hamburgers name their daughter?
Patty.

What town in England makes terrible sandwiches?
Oldham.

Knock Knock.
  Who's there?
Gorilla.
  Gorilla who?
Gorilla me a hamburger,
  I'm hungry!

Terry: I understand fish is
  brain food.
Brad: Yes, I eat it all the time.
Terry: Well, there goes
  another scientific theory.

18

How do you insult a hamburger patty?
  Call it a meatball.

What do cats put on their hamburgers?
  Mouse-tard.

What was the hamburger's favorite fairy tale?
  Hansel and Gristle.

What did the hot dog say when it won the race?
  I'm a wiener!

Where do hamburgers go on New Year's Eve?
  To a meat ball.

Why do the hamburgers beat the hot dogs at every sport they play?
  Because the hot dogs are the wurst.

How many chickens does it take to serve 10 people?
  Chickens aren't good at serving. Better get waiters and waitresses.

CONDIMENT JOKES

What did the mayonnaise say to the refrigerator? Close the door, I'm dressing.

What did one tomato say to the other tomato? You run ahead and I'll ketchup.

Why was the mayonnaise late for the game? Because it was dressing.

Did you hear about the man who was so absentminded he poured ketchup on his shoelaces and tied knots in his spaghetti?

MORE FOOD JOKES

Why did the man eat dinner at the bank? He wanted to eat rich food.

What do ants put on their pizza? Ant-chovies.

Why is a chef mean? Because he beats the eggs, mashes the potatoes, and whips the cream.

What does a shark eat with peanut butter? Jellyfish.

What does a lion eat when he goes to a restaurant? The waiter.

What has four legs and flies? A picnic table.

Did you hear about the outlaw who's so tough that when he wants a cup of tea, he swallows a mouthful of water and a tea bag and sits on a hot stove until the water boils?

What do frogs drink at picnics?
Croak-a-cola.

How do Martians drink their tea?
In flying saucers.

What do prizefighters bring to a picnic?
A box lunch.

What happens if you eat yeast and shoe polish?
In the morning, you'll rise and shine.

How do you serve a football player his clam chowder?
In a soup-er bowl.

What happened when the diver fell 100 feet into a glass of root beer?
Nothing. It was a soft drink.

Knock Knock.
Who's there?
Justin.
Justin who?
Justin time for supper.

What's a tree's favorite drink?
Root beer.

23

About Patrick Girouard:

Patrick Girouard has been illustrating books for almost 15 years but still looks remarkably lifelike. He loves reading, movies, coffee, robots, a beautiful red-haired lady named Rita, and especially his sons, Marc and Max. Here's an interesting fact: A dog named Sam lives under his drawing board. You can visit him (Patrick, not Sam) at  www.pgirouard.com.

About Pam Rosenberg:

Pam Rosenberg is a former junior high school teacher and corporate trainer. She currently works as an author, editor, and the mother of Sarah and Jake. She took on this project as a service to all her fellow parents of young children. At least now their kids will have lots of jokes to choose from when looking for the one they will tell their parents over and over and over again!